RHINE ARMY SUMMER

◆

The (not too serious) memoirs of a young Royal Artillery Officer in Germany in the Nineteen Sixties

Colin Boxall-Hunt

iUniverse, Inc.
New York Lincoln Shanghai

RHINE ARMY SUMMER

The (not too serious) memoirs of a young Royal Artillery Officer in Germany in the Nineteen Sixties

iUniverse books may be ordered through booksellers or by contacting:

iUniverse
2021 Pine Lake Road, Suite 100
Lincoln, NE 68512
www.iuniverse.com
1-800-Authors (1-800-288-4677)

ISBN: 978-0-595-48300-6 (pbk)
ISBN: 978-0-595-60388-6 (ebk)

Printed in the United States of America

This book is dedicated to Patsy Ayerst, who rescued, consoled, and healed me and switched on the light, and to Brigadier Ian Stansfield, OLM, ever a staunch and loyal comrade from the start. *"NOLI ILLEGITIMATI CARBORUNDUM!"*

Contents

1

Arrival

Summer was well underway in the British Army of the Rhine when Second Lieutenant Algernon Charles "Warty" Nasty-Farting, one year or so "fresh out of the egg", and recently having finished his Young Officers' course at the Royal School of Artillery and been posted to a Regiment based in Sennelager, North-West Germany, armed with 8" Howitzers and "Honest John" missiles, arrived on the chartered "Air Trooper" at RAF Gutersloh after an uncomfortable flight from Luton. He was met, without apparent enthusiasm, by a Subaltern of his new Regiment, his senior by possibly two years—a vast gulf. This guide somewhat curtly led him (naturally—it was late at night) to a small and battered short-wheelbase Landrover, and, with some difficulty, Warty loaded his bags and clambered aboard. At least, he thought, it was not raining at the moment, although the night air was chilly. His guide, of course, sat in the front passenger seat, protected from the wind.

An hour or so later Warty was decanted at the entrance to the Officers' Mess Block in the former German Army Wehrmacht barracks now occupied by his new Regiment. In the hope of, perhaps, a meal and a drink, Warty quickly followed a taciturn Scottish Mess Sergeant to his allocated room, quickly washed and changed, and repaired downstairs to where the sounds of revelry seemed promising.

Alas, Warty's hopes for solid and liquid sustenance were unrealised, for it was swiftly revealed to him that all newly joining Officers must be given (more accurately *undergo*) a "Regimental Welcome". This consisted of promoting their embarrassment and confusing them about the real identities of Regimental personalities. Thus, the distinguished-looking gent to whom Warty was introduced as the Commanding Officer was, in reality, an elderly Quartermaster, who sternly terrified Warty about what would be expected of him. The part of the Colonel's lady was taken by a cheerful, full-bosomed, willing and good-humoured girl, who was, in fact, one of the local Army schoolteachers, who had been persuaded to put on an act of seduction. Luckily, even inexperienced Warty realised this was hardly likely to be the behaviour of his Commanding Officer's wife, or, if it was, the consequences of succumbing would be unthinkable, so beat a hasty retreat in the direction of an apparent Padre (in real life a senior Captain in borrowed "dog collar"), whose lisp and limp-wristed demeanour served to further arouse Warty's suspicion about exactly what sort of Regiment he had joined. However, having resisted all the pitfalls, and being adjudged worthy of joining the Mess, Warty finally managed a few hours' sleep, and on rising next morning, eventually found the Dining Room (his guide and mentor being nowhere to be seen) and, fortified by his first proper Mess breakfast, sallied forth in his new military finery to find RHQ and report to the (genuine) Commanding Officer, via the Adjutant (whom, it transpired, he had last met the previous evening, dressed and acting as a Mess waiter). After a formal welcome, the Colonel told Warty that he was to be given command of 15 soldiers and an 8" toad. Recoiling from the mental image, and struggling not to giggle (Instruction at Sandhurst had been lacking at how to cope with large green amphibians), Warty finally realised that the Colonel meant a towed 8" howitzer, the tracked self-propelled version being not yet available to British Regiments.

2

Warty starts to learn his Craft

And so, Warty settled into the routine of peacetime soldiering in BAOR consisting of "dry" and Command Post communication exercises, live firing of his howitzer on the NATO Ranges in the far North of Germany, regular training and inspections, courses to further and improve his military education, and complemented, of course, by a good social life, both formal and informal, centered usually round the Mess. He grew to know his soldiers and practised the art of Gunnery. He learned to listen to, respect, and appreciate the advice of those older and wiser men, not necessarily always superior in rank, but often vastly so in knowledge and experience. He took pains invariably to consult, when appropriate, and listen to the Warrant Officers, principally his Battery Sergeant-Major, "Bobo" Charmes, and Senior NCOs, in particular Keith "Monkey" Lawrance, a heroic and much liked, although notably ugly—hence his nickname—figure, his Battery Quartermaster Sergeant. It became Warty's custom, once accepted as a young Officer (a "Rupert" in Regimental parlance, who wasn't too proud to listen and learn), to visit, whenever possible, the "old and Bold" Battery characters like Monkey to receive such nuggets of accumulated wisdom as they saw fit to disburse. Indeed, Warty would often escape from the rigours of duty to take shelter in Monkey's Equipment Store, which had been established in one of the cellars below the Battery's accommodation and office block. Here, he could be given advice on the conduct proper for young Officers, and since he had shown a willingness to listen and learn, Monkey took him "under his wing", and tried as far as possible to keep him from trouble, and steer him clear of the wrath of his superiors consequent upon any peccadillo inseparable from the life of an inexperienced Regimental Officer.

Thus it was one day when Warty was again sheltering in Monkey's Store, when a hapless new recruit from a newly arrived Draft tapped on the door to the Store and nervously requested certain items of clothing. Monkey's lip curled with disdain. Like any BQMS, he was not renowned for his kindly disposition, nor for his generosity in dispensing equipment entrusted to his care by an ever ungrateful and watchful MoD, as his mantra to those unwise enough to request such bounty pointed out. "See that sign above the door!" he bellowed at the hapless recruit. "It says 'Stores'—which means that I stores kit! If I was supposed to hand it out to clowns like you, it would say 'Issues', wouldn't it? Now, 'oppit!" And with that he retired, again triumphant, to his favourite corner, where his trusty but truly horrible storeman, 'Arry "Maggot" Perkins, could soothe him with an outsize mug of "NATO Standard" (white with two sugars) tea.

"Never you mind Q," said Maggot. "Remember Kenya?"

"Aagh," said Monkey, reflectively picking his teeth. "Them was the days."

Warty, sensing a yarn, came closer. He had heard the story, before, after dinner in the Mess, and perhaps embroidered just a little over the Port, because it was a regimental favourite, but here was a chance to hear it from the chief protagonist. Some years earlier, in the 1950's, the regiment was based in Kenya, when an urgent call came from the Higher Beings that a (Native) Infantry Regiment of African Rifles had mutinied, and that the Regiment was to deploy with all despatch to investigate and take necessary action. The bulk of the Regiment therefore deployed post haste, leaving only rear parties in barracks. "X" Battery's rear party consisted of Monkey, Maggot, and one sergeant and six Gunners as a Guard. Hearing that the mutineers were close, the Guard rapidly and sensibly retired to the Guardroom, where the sergeant issued each man with a rifle and 100 rounds of live ammunition. Monkey, being principally concerned with the safety of his jealously hoarded stock of equipment, for which he had signed, barricaded Maggot and himself in his Store, having first ensured that adequate supplies of "Tusker" lager were to hand (storekeeping in Kenya being an especially thirst-provoking activity).

On the approach of the native horde, Monkey, with loud and enraged imprecations about "Thieving Black B—s after his kit", dissuaded any attempt to enter his beloved Store by creating through the single small barred window such a barrage of foul oaths and empty beer bottles that the mutineers fled in panic, while Maggot was driven almost to a sodden despair in his attempt to maintain adequate ammunition, Monkey declining, like a good and thrifty soldier, to waste good beer by hurling full bottles.

Luckily, the situation was resolved by the return of "J" battery after a successful operation. They rounded up the bedraggled and subdued mutineers, and, after a Summary Court Martial had found them guilty, hanged the two ringleaders from a convenient Masasa Tree near the Guardroom, thereby establishing Moral Superiority, and re-establishing Good Military Discipline. The thirty or so remaining mutineers were disarmed and crammed into the three standard size (6' x 8') cells in the Guardroom.

On seeing this, an enraged Monkey emerged from his Store, blinking in the sunlight, vowing revenge on his enemies, and leaving a somewhat unsteady Maggot to polish and burnish as usual—and apply a new coat of Army "Red Lead" paint to the floor of the store. Deciding that the ex-mutineers were dirty and smelly in addition to their other faults, Monkey turned the high-pressure fire hoses on them in the cells, between long bursts of cold water showering them with "Dettol", and wielding a bass broom to good effect.

There were no further outbreaks of ill-discipline in any of the Kenyan Regiments, and Monkey even managed to force down a "Tusker" or six that evening in the Sergeants' Mess to celebrate a job well done. Maggot, on the other hand, felt ill for a week, and couldn't even enter the NAAFI Canteen, let along enjoy a glass of beer. He didn't get much sympathy, though.

"So, Sir", finished Monkey to Warty, "learn the lesson about how to treat Black fellers."

3

An Inspection

On a future occasion, Warty was once again sheltering in Monkey's Store, hoping for more advice, and possibly another yarn, when an urgent message arrived by runner from BSM Charmes that the Commanding Officer had descended from his Godlike vastness in RHQ, and was en route to make a surprise inspection of the Store. Warty rose, ready to flee, but Monkey's stern injunction to "Stay still, Sir, keep quiet, say nothing, and watch" kept him in his place in a corner of the Store, while Maggot put the kettle on to boil and Monkey went to meet the Colonel and usher him down to the Store for a restorative cup of tea. The Colonel, having ascertained that the gallon flagon of MoD issue Rum (for distribution only in the worst of conditions and in circumstances minutely prescribed by Queen's Regulations, the Army Act 1955 and Tablets of Stone) contained only pure Rum, undiluted by cold tea (perish the thought of that particular Old Soldier's Ruse), and having congratulated Monkey on the gleaming perfection of the "G1098" stores laid out on the racking, the Colonel, followed by the motley gang of Me-toos, moved down the corridor.

After about ten yards, he stopped in front of a securely barred door to the next cellar, painted bright red and festooned with numerous warning signs surmounted by a "Skull and Crossbones" to this effect: "KEEP OUT, DOE HEATING CELLAR, NO ENTRY, HIGH VOLTAGE ELECTRICITY, LEBENSGEFAHR! DO NOT ENTER ON RISK OF DEATH."

"Right!" said the Colonel, undismayed and undeterred, "BQMS, get it open. I want to see inside!"

"Sorry, Sir, can't," said Monkey, "It's a DOE cellar—says so, don't it? Very dangerous. Not at all suitable or proper for Officers. 'Sides, it's probably full of spiders and dust and such—bound to ruin our toecaps." And his face set in that rigid determined look the regiment knew so well.

"I don't care!" said the Colonel. "I WANT IT OPEN NOW!"

HMV must be obeyed. Maggot was sent scuttling off for a rusty vast key, and with much groaning of hinges and mutinous muttering from Monkey, the door swung open and the Colonel stepped in. To be greeted by …

A duplicate gleaming mirror image of Monkey's Store, complete with shining red-leaded floor and racks of burnished immaculate GI098 stores—another Battery's worth.

The Colonel fixed Monkey with a steely gimlet eye. "BQMS," he said, "I've a feeling that I don't really want to know, but, first, Why?"

"Aah, well Sir," said Monkey, "in my real Store, I keep my proper kit, for inspection, checking, like. In this store I keep the kit I lets the beggars take out on exercise. They do get it dirty, Sir, and dent it and spoil it!"

"Hmm," said the Colonel. "How?"

"Well, Sir, there's ways known only to BQMS's—Board of Survey kit, like, which magically returns, kit that you write off, Sir, and which is repaired, and a network of exchanges for favours with other BQMS's in the Regiment, and chums in other Regiments in the garrison, Sir. Every little helps, like the old lady said as she pee'd in the sea!"

"Harrumph!" grunted the Colonel. "Come on, young Nasty-Farting, let's get out of this nest of thieves and go to the Mess for a cup of tea. I need it!"

So did Warty, but he stayed and had one with Monkey while Maggot repaired the damage to his toecaps and removed the spiders from his turn-ups.

4

A Border Patrol

In those times of increased tasks, shrinking drafts from the Training Regiments, and reduced manpower, the newly arrived soldier allocated by the BSM to the not unduly onerous post of BQMS Storeman was usually either the young and hopeful type, mentally or physically less suited to any other role in the Battery such as Gun Detachment, Driver, Signaller, etc, or the "Old and Bold" Veteran, no longer so active, but having a wealth of experience and native cunning. "Maggot" Perkins was one such. Truly horrible to observe, unsavoury of habit and aspect, his wizened stature and leathery skin attested to the suns and winds of many seasons of worldwide campaigns in Her Majesty's Service. His harsh racking cough caused by thousands of sneaked "drags" could be heard around the Barracks from Reveille to NAAFI-Break and after.

Unfailingly and annoyingly chirpy, he would invariably boldly introduce himself to any Inspecting General on "Admin Day" with a grubby outstretched paw and a cheery "Mornin Sah!" or "'Arry Perkins—Old Soldier, Long Service, 'Ot Climates." Sometimes, the General would concede defeat with a good grace and compliment Maggot on being able to stand upright despite the weight of campaign medals on his chest. More usually, the General would recoil in horror from the appalling spectacle.

The Regiment was stationed in BAOR, to safeguard the Frontiers of the Free West. Its barracks was close to the East German (or "Inner German" as Warty was told to call it) border. One of the tasks was to carry out regular patrols along the Border to see if there had been any change to the wire fortifications and minefields that the East Germans had positioned to keep their people in, or evidence of incursion into West Germany by armed forces or refugees.

A Patrol normally consisted of a (fairly junior) Officer, an experienced NCO to keep him in order, and about 10 soldiers, all mounted in 3 or 4 Landrovers or "Ferret" armoured cars.

In 1965, Warty was summoned to the "Kremlin" or "Headshed" as the Subalterns disrespectfully referred to Regimental Headquarters, where he was tasked by the Adjutant to deploy a Border Patrol from his battery.

Panicking only slightly, Warty sought the advice of Battery Sergeant Major Charmes, and four days later set forth, with his warning ringing in his ears about a previous patrol that had negligently allowed a radio and two weapons to be stolen from the vehicles while in an overnight laager, and that the District Court Martial of the Patrol Commander, like him a Lieutenant, was imminent.

One of the great joys of a Patrol was that they were billeted overnight in farms in the small villages along the Border, where they were sure of a warm welcome from the Farmer, and the ever-present hope of an even warmer welcome from the farmer's daughter, eager (they hoped!) to acquire in the traditional manner a British passport and a young British Officer as a protector.

So, full of trepidation about all these possibilities, Warty selected a farm for their first overnight stop, informed the farmer that they would occupy his barn for two nights or so, and retired to draft his first report to RHQ, leaving the detail of settling in the Patrol to the tender and vastly more experienced mercies of his Patrol NCO, Sgt. Deamer, who, wary of the fact that the BSM had made up patrol numbers by including Maggot, gave him an extra strict briefing about the risk of locals trying to creep up and steal their equipment or rations. The sentries were therefore set to patrol with fixed bayonets (live ammunition which they carried "in bulk" being considered "de trop" so close to the Border).

At about 2 a.m. on a dark morning, Warty was woken by a loud shriek, followed by a steady moaning and a curious clanking noise that he could not readily identify. Having stood the Patrol to and therefore confident of the backup of the fierce Sgt. Deamer and his 10 gallant heroes, he investigated, to find Maggot, incoherent with rage and pride, having pinned to the barn door a scrawny-looking local spotty youth, by the expedient of thrusting his bayonet through the youth's coat, narrowly and luckily missing his flesh. The moaning came from the petrified German, the clanking noise from the chains which Maggot had found somewhere in the barn, and with which he had completely swathed his captive from neck to ankle, rendering impossible any movement apart from a pitiful twitching (hence the clanking).

"Gottim Sir!" yelled Maggot. "Caught the beggar sneaking round the back of your truck trying to get in. Bet he was after your radio and chocolate biscuits, Sir! Please can I stick him a bit, Sir, just a bit, just to learn him!"

With some difficulty Warty managed to dissuade him, and with Sgt. Deamer's aid released the prisoner from his fetters, summoned the local German Police, and handed over the thoroughly cowed spotty youth to them.

The next day as they set off, the local Burgermeister arrived, bearing gifts of Beer and Sausage for the patrol. The spotty prisoner was apparently a well-known local ne're-do-well, suspected of many crimes including arson. Maggot was fêted as a Hero and enjoined to return to the village.

After a successful patrol they returned to barracks. Warty never did get to meet the farmer's daughter!

5

Warty Goes Sailing

The Colonel was pleased with young Warty, who appeared to have settled in well to Regimental life. Accordingly, the Colonel decided to reward him with attendance at an offshore sailing course at the British Kiel Yacht Club, based in the Southern Baltic, North of Hamburg.

The BKYC was actually a unit of BAOR, headed as Chief Instructor by a Royal Engineers Captain, and staffed by NCOs from various Regiments. They were all keen and very proficient yachtsmen, and ran courses throughout the year for members of BAOR Units, many of them young Officers, who would then be encouraged to bring soldiers from their own Units for adventurous training expeditions on the ten yachts with which the BKYC was equipped. These yachts had been "liberated" at the end of WW2 from the Germans, and although engineless, were well maintained, and considered to be ideal for teaching soldiers the rudiments of nautical lore including navigation and seamanship in the tide-less waters of the Baltic, and in and around the islands and harbours of the South Danish coast.

So Warty attended a two-week course, passed the final practical and theory exams, and returned to Sennelager looking forward to taking the first party from his Regiment back to Kiel for further sail training. While on his course, he met two Officers who were to play an important part in his life. The first, Captain (Quartermaster) Ron Howard, he had met before, on the night of his arrival at the Officers' Mess. Ron, the Quartermaster of a Unit in the same Garrison, had been the one posing as Warty's Commanding Officer. He was a calm, mild-mannered, pipe-smoking Officer, of vast experience, who had Quarter-mastered from Hong Kong to Benghazi, and all stations in between. He had been happily married for many years to the pleasant-natured and cat-loving Pauline, the School Secretary at the Sennelager Forces' school. Ron's other pride and joy was his car, a sleek diesel Mercedes-Benz, for which he and Pauline had scrimped and saved for many years, and upon the bodywork of which Ron had lavished many hours of labour to maintain its glossy and pristine condition.

The other old chum Warty had met had been at Sandhurst at the same time. He was a Royal Military Police Officer, whose nickname was "The Black Dwarf" and whose real name was mercifully lost in the mists of time and legend, RMP Officers not being universally loved or appreciated. However, the three of them got on very well indeed, and enjoyed sailing so much that on return to Sennelager they decided one night over supper in Ron's Married Quarter to form a small syndicate, to buy a yacht together, and share all costs. Warty was elected to head the syndicate, complete all necessary research, and come up with a plan.

And so he did. A formal agreement was drawn up between the three partners, the yacht (a 26', six berth *Heavenly Twins* offshore cruising catamaran with a powerful inboard-mounted outboard engine) was chosen and purchased, and a berth for her arranged near Portsmouth. Not ideal, perhaps, for owners based in Germany, but convenient enough for all three to enjoy sailing her during periods of leave.

After two years, however, the partners decided that a berth in the South of France would be even more convenient and congenial, and Warty had read of several new Marinas under construction in the Camargue region that sounded eminently suitable. They therefore decided, and arranged leave accordingly to move their yacht, now Christened *Sundance* down to the Mediterranean in stages, using the French inland waterways where possible. Stage One was to sail *Sundance* over the English Channel, through the Brittany canal system, and down the coast of the Bay of Biscay to the port of Royan, at the mouth if the River Gironde, and there to overwinter her ashore, ready for Stage Two the following Spring, when a new leave year would be available.

To implement good administration, it was decided that Warty and the Black Dwarf would crew the yacht through the canals and down the coast, with QM Ron "shadowing" them by car, going ahead when necessary to restock with essential supplies such as fuel, wine and food, and meeting at a pre-arranged RV each evening.

This, in principle, was an excellent idea, and worked well for the first two weeks or so, by which time *Sundance* was well on her way across Brittany. At this stage, QM Ron and the Black Dwarf decided that a change of role would be in order, so Ron joined Warty to crew the yacht, and the Black Dwarf drove off one morning in Ron's cherished Merc, with Warty's strict orders to meet that evening at the RV with a chicken and fresh vegetables for dinner.

At about 4 p.m., after a tiring day opening and closing lock gates, Warty and Ron were enjoying a mug of tea in the cockpit, when Warty saw in the distance a small, bedraggled and dejected looking figure standing alone on the tow path, surrounded by plastic carrier bags. As they approached, it turned out to be the Black Dwarf, who climbed aboard, apparently close to tears, as he poured out his tale of woe to an increasingly stricken and aghast Ron, whose beloved car was nowhere to be seen.

Having completed his shopping, The Black Dwarf had stopped for a very brief coffee and cognac in a café next to the small supermarket. On leaving, he noticed ominous black smoke coming from the engine of the Merc. Bravely but foolishly, he opened the bonnet, which, of course allowed oxygen access to the smouldering diesel from a loose fuel pipe. More smoke and flames followed, but he had the presence of mind to grab the fire extinguisher with which the cautious Ron had equipped his car. The printed instructions being to bang the release catch on a hard surface, the Black Dwarf had used the nearest such surface, which happened to be the highly polished wing of the Merc, resulting in deep dents when the wretched extinguisher had failed to function on the first bang. The smoke grew denser and, finally, to the noisy glee of a gang of Frenchmen who had erupted from the café but stood well back to watch, he had brought the fire under control. He then arranged for a local garage to collect the car and put repairs to the engine and bodywork in hand, and made his unhappy way on foot back to the towpath to await his fate—which, thought QM Ron, he richly deserved, as he covered the Black Dwarf in foam from a spare extinguisher and pushed him into the canal to clean him up prior to fishing him out, drying him and forgiving him. Warty tactfully got on with cooking the chicken and fresh vegetables and testing the wine, not entirely trusting the Black Dwarf's taste in such things (although his courage was beyond doubt).

6

Warty all at Sea

Early the next Spring the three partners and an extra crewman drove in Ron's repaired Mercedes to Royan from Sennelager and arranged for *Sundance* to be craned into the water and continue her journey to the Mediterranean. Soon she was making her way up river.

The five warships of the standing NATO Squadron based in Bordeaux sailed majestically in line astern down the river Gironde towards the Bay of Biscay and the open Atlantic. In the other direction puttered the 26' catamaran *Sundance*, with her intrepid skipper Warty (in his other persona of "Colin the Red, Searover") at the helm, struggling to make good a speed of 4 knots against the flow of the river, and intent on reaching the entrance to the French canal system at Bordeaux and the next stage of an epic voyage through the French waterways to the Mediterranean.

Warty's crew, sometimes sullen and mutinous, but today bright and breezy, consisted of his old accomplice Dave, known as "The Black Dwarf", A 5'2" killer from the skies, who was an administrator par excellence, a very decent inshore pilot, and an ideal foil for Warty's bluff, hearty, and sometimes misguided good nature. Where Warty was medium tall, plump, blond, cheerily red-faced, placid and trusting, The Black Dwarf was short, lean, swarthy, suspicious, and of a jaundiced nature. The third crewman was another Dave, L.Bdr.Rooke, an NCO recruited for the trip ("volunteered"—as he put it) from amongst the ranks of Warty's battery in BAOR. Rooke was there to add cheerful muscle in times of stress. 6'5" tall, blond-haired and tireless, his happy English disposition was a credit to his race and regiment. The fourth member was of course, QM Ron.

As the NATO Squadron approached, Warty remembered that nautical honours must be paid by "dipping his ensign" in salute to each warship. This, on such a small yacht as *Sundance*, he could accomplish easily enough by reaching a long arm behind him to the flagstaff. However, inspired by the wish to be a touch more formal, and with the hint of a wicked twinkle in his eye, he dispatched

Black Dave to the foredeck, there to act out the role of a Royal Marine Band, and mutely play anthems as the ensign was dipped to each warship in turn. This had the most gratifying effect. The eagle-eyed duty officer on watch on each warship sent a seaman racing to his own ship's ensign to dip in response, as custom dictated.

Five times Warty somewhat languidly but smartly dipped the Red Ensign. Five times the Black Dwarf crashed imaginary cymbals, blew imaginary trumpets, and presented arms with the boat hook. Five times a sailor of the NATO Squadron scurried aft to dip his country's ensign to salute the tiny *Sundance*.

Maritime honour was satisfied.

7

A Haunted Night (Deeper into France)

Having safely navigated *Sundance* into the French canal system, it was time for a crew change. Black Dave was needed in the UK to assist with some nefarious and mysterious business in the marshes of the South Coast, and L/Bdr Rooke had to return to his military duties in BAOR, as had QM Ron.

Warty had, therefore, enlisted the help of his younger brother Brian. A serving Royal Navy Officer, Brian was determined to disprove the old adage beloved of yachtsmen that "The three most useless things on a small yacht are an umbrella, a stepladder, and a Naval Officer". And so he did, as we shall see. In true nautical fashion, he had grown quite a respectable "full set"—i.e. Beard—which made him resemble very closely indeed a younger version of King George V, complete with piercing blue eyes. "I don't know if he terrifies the French," muttered Warty, misquoting one of his military heroes, The Duke of Wellington, "but, by Golly, he terrifies me!"

The first few days motoring steadily south and west went well, with both brothers taking their turn at the helm, cooking and cleaning. Then the weather changed. It became glacial, with a cutting icy North wind driving snow and sleet showers. Steering in the open cockpit became a misery, even for the sea-hardened Brian, who, muffled in numerous layers of clothing and a thick woollen helmet, developed frost and icicles in his beard, dispersed briefly only when Warty passed up the companionway yet another steaming mug of cocoa or soup from the galley below, in which he had taken momentary refuge.

The nights, normally berthed snugly alongside the canal or riverbank, were bearable since they had a small gas powered heater, although Warty remarked cynically that if it failed, they could always keep their hands or feet warm by putting them inside the fridge!

One dark and stormy evening, about 200 miles through the canal system, they moored up earlier than usual. It had been a long, cold, hard day. Leaping onto the towpath to drive in the mooring stakes was especially hazardous and difficult because a sharp and swift drop in temperature had frozen the ground hard and made it extremely slippery. Brian did a superb and professional job, however, and made all secure while Warty, cook for the day, put on a plump chicken to roast for their dinner. It was one of his favourite dishes and he invariably cooked it well.

That night our heroes prepared to enter their sleeping bags replete with chicken and good red wine, until Brian returned from his customary "First Lieutenant's evening rounds"—i.e. a check that all was still well above. He reported quite calmly to Warty that they were moored close to a ruined castle, which loomed over them, illuminated spasmodically by a fitful moon shining through the scudding clouds. Having decided that the castle was either haunted, or, alternatively, the lair of French Bandits (prejudice dies hard in the Royal Navy), he commenced to take what he insisted were just "wise and seaman like precautions".

These precautions consisted of setting traps and tripwires on the upper deck and in the cockpit, to give audible warning, locking and barricading the companionway hatch, and placing close to hand the heavy mallet used to drive in the mooring stakes, a large and fearsome-looking knife that he had acquired somewhere on the way, and the boathook, the end of which he had sharpened into a spear. Thus reassured of the safety of ship and crew, the night proceeded, the peace disturbed only by Warty's stentorian snoring that, in itself, Brian thought, was sufficient to deter the boldest Frenchman—which it possibly did, because when Brian made his morning inspection to disarm his traps and prepare to sail, he saw footprints in the light snow covering of the footpath, but none on the deck of *Sundance*. Proud that his precautions had been effective, yet a little dismayed that he hadn't caught a French bandit, Brian called for a hearty breakfast, which Warty, invariably cheerful, supplied before they set off once more.

8

Finally to the Med

After another crew change, the Black Dwarf again replacing Warty's brother Brian who had been summoned back to Naval duty, *Sundance* continued on her way south through the French waterways. Although still shorthanded, two agile males were just sufficient to work her through the locks, finally emerging from the inland waterway system via the very scenic Canal du Midi, and thence to the Mediterranean port of Sete, where a crane was available to hoist *Sundance's* mast again. A few days were spent in port, rigging and restocking her, with many complaints from the Black Dwarf about the heartless cruelty of Warty in making him ascend the mast to check the halyards and fittings at the top. It was still very cold, and he did this in the teeth of a developing Mistral wind. However, *Sundance* was soon again rigged and ready, and even though still shorthanded, the intrepid pair decided to put to sea before the weather got even worse, and make for their planned destination of the new Marina at Port Camargue, just ten or so sea miles along the coast to the east.

They had a good fast run with a stiff breeze from their port side, Warty navigating and manning the helm and the Black Dwarf assuming his usual role of trusted inshore pilot. They had already found from the pilot books and local sailing instructions that the offshore entrance to Port Camargue was indicated by a buoy with a single flashing white light, and that they would then have to pass between a green starboard light and a red port light marking the actual entrance to the harbour.

About halfway to their destination, as night was falling, the wind started to pick up, until *Sundance* was surfing down the steep following seas. Both Warty and the Black Dwarf felt uncomfortable with this, so they shortened sail to just a storm jib and a deeply reefed mainsail, and maintained a close and hopeful watch, with the Black Dwarf stationed in the bows with his military binoculars, hampered by his slightly defective right eye, which had only partial sight following an accident in Saudi Arabia. However, his sight was good enough to spot lights ahead, and he reported to Warty in great joy: "White light dead ahead—possibly the buoy! And red and green light to Port—possibly the harbour entrance!" But their joy and relief was short-lived when an orange light joined the green and red, and all three showed in sequence! They realised that they were traffic signals in Port Camargue High Street! Just then, the offshore marker buoy with its flashing white light surged past at a great rate of knots. They made a smartly executed turn to port, dropped and secured the mainsail, started the engine, and followed the correct course (due north) towards Port Camargue, passing between the correct harbour entrance lights, which became clearly visible as they approached, and into the calm water of the Marina, with its brilliantly illuminated pontoons, the lights of which had been obscured at sea by the high harbour walls.

This was probably not the first time that mariners had mistaken shore lights for leading lights into a safe haven, but unusual for a traffic signal to be to blame. However, all was well that ended well and after snugging *Sundance* down in her safe Marina berth, a few whiskies were taken to soothe and restore ragged nerve endings. The Mistral could now howl its worst, and so it did, but Warty and the Black Dwarf were oblivious to it. The partners kept *Sundance* in Port Camargue for the next three years, and many more adventures ensued, but the telling of these must await a future occasion.

9

Warty's Oilrig

After several tours of duty as a Regimental Officer, Warty was selected to go "on Loan" to the Forces of HM The Sultan of Oman, whom the British Government were helping to subdue a Communist-inspired revolt in the South of his country. After several months of active service deployed directing artillery fire against the terrorist gangs, Warty was one morning summoned to his Brigadier's office in the Headquarters. An oilrig platform had been wrenched adrift from its normal mooring in the Arabian Gulf by pirates. They were towing the rig southwards using a powerful and heavily armed tug, with the aim of selling the multi-million dollar equipment to any unscrupulous undertaking—or country—with enough money to buy it.

Unluckily for the pirates, however, the tow had parted and the rig had drifted with the current, and was now fast aground on the Omani coast, some 500 miles north of the Headquarters where Warty was based. With the warning that the pirates were still lurking close to the stranded rig with their heavily armed tug-boat, and were certain to resist violently any attempt to deprive them of the oil-rig, the Brigadier ordered Warty to assemble an "ad hoc" force, arrange helicopter transport to take them and sufficient stores and weaponry, and go to the site of the stranded oilrig, defeat any attempt of the pirates to interfere, and get a line from the shore to aboard the oilrig to make good a legal salvage claim on the behalf of the Government of Oman, the procedure recognised in international law.

With help of the administrative expertise of the Black Dwarf, who was serving in the same Headquarters, Warty assembled a small but potent task force of a sergeant and 20 soldiers, with what he estimated would be sufficient stores, weapons and ammunition to do the job.

The Sultan's Air Force supplied helicopters to ferry them to the salvage site, where Warty established a base in the sand dunes along the shore, screened from the clearly visible pirate tug, but from where he could keep the stranded oilrig under observation, hard aground about 500 yards offshore in shallow water.

Warty could clearly see the surf bursting over the deck. After a sparse but satisfying meal cooked over a driftwood fire, and having set sentries to guard against a surprise raid by the pirates, the group settled down to rest. Tomorrow, Warty was aware, might prove testing.

Before dawn, Warty was awake long before Sgt Ibrahim roused the soldiers, all devout Baluchi Muslims, for the first of their daily prayer sessions. A chill breeze came off the sea and a slight sea-fret mist obscured the pirate tugboat, although the stark lines of the stranded oilrig were clear against the sky as the sun rose. Warty continued to ponder the problem of how to get a line to the rig.

The Brigadier, however, had chosen with care. He knew more than many suspected. He was well aware that Warty was not only a powerful swimmer, but also a trained and experienced boat-handler, and a highly experienced and well-qualified underwater diver—the ideal candidate, in fact, to overcome surf, tide, and current to reach the oilrig and achieve its security, as well as having the military expertise to defend it and repel any attempt by pirates, however well armed, to disrupt his operation. And so it transpired. Deciding to seize the initiative, Warty engaged the pirate tug with his 81mm Mortar (as a Gunner, he had always insisted that this weapon was far too good for Infantry). With remarkable forbearance, he resisted the temptation to drop a bomb directly down the tug's funnel, even though he was quite capable of such accuracy. The pirates, of course, very soon "got the message", and steamed off towards the distant horizon, to the frustration of Warty's men who had been rather enjoying engaging them with machine guns which also formed part of the arsenal. Bloodthirsty lot, when aroused, Baluchis. Warty, having tied a thin "messenger" cable round his waist, swam out through the surf to the stranded oilrig, and used the messenger to haul across from the shore a heavier cable, thus making good the salvage claim, which he reinforced by hoisting the Omani flag from the highest point of the rig that he could reach. Sergeant Ibrahim and several of his more adventurous soldiers now used the main cable to get out to the oilrig, which, despite having been fairly systematically plundered by the pirates, still contained many objects of interest and value, such as beds, radios and household goods. All these were ferried back through the surf to the camp, and claimed by Warty's soldiers as legitimate plunder of war. Warty himself found the energy to launch a badly damaged inflatable boat, which, once ashore, he managed to repair and eventually recover to HQ. It finally ended up as tender to *Sundance*.

About a week later a large tug hired by the Omani Government arrived to salvage the oilrig and take it in tow back to its proper location. Warty's party was recovered back to HQ, where they were all congratulated by the Brigadier. The pirates, thoroughly discouraged, never returned. Warty had won—and was in due course awarded a little strip of coloured ribbon to wear on his uniform. He remains inordinately proud of it, and later returned to Sennelager.

10

A Nightmare for the NAAFI Manager

(The Naval, Army, and Air Force Institute provides shops for Service personnel on a worldwide basis)

Shortly after Warty's return in triumph to HQ, after the incident of "Warty's Oilrig", he was given permission for his wife to come out to Oman for a short visit. Although normally an unaccompanied tour of duty for the whole two-year period of secondment to HM The Sultan's Forces, these visits were very occasionally permitted if suitable accommodation was available and air transport could be arranged. With these necessities in place, Warty's wife, a forceful, vociferous, exuberant and somewhat excitable half Austrian, half Hungarian Viennese PhD with a Doctorate in Anthropology, had arrived, and taken up residence in the bungalow of a civilian contractor who had returned to the UK on long leave. The Brigadier, partly as a reward for Warty's capture of the oilrig, gave him permission to live off camp in the bungalow until required for operations, coming into camp each day for duty. Corporal Said Mohammed, Warty's driver, was one of the Pakistani Baluch soldiers who served in the Sultan's Army on contract, and had been in Warty's force that recaptured the oilrig. Another of his duties was to act as driver and escort for Dr. D. (Warty's wife) if she needed transport. (European wives in those days being prohibited from driving themselves).

On the RAF base close to Warty's HQ there was a NAAFI shop which stocked the essentials of English life overseas—tea, marmalade, Marmite, Mars bars, etc, none of which were available in the local Omani Arab *souk* (market). The manager was an Indian Hindu, a courteous and inoffensive little gentleman who served his customers well, and was much liked.

One morning the Brigadier summoned Warty to his office. Hoping it wasn't another Special Operation, Warty rushed to obey, to find the Brigadier trying to calm the RAF Officer commanding the base, who was in a state of great agitation.

"Warty!" growled the Brigadier, "Get up to the RAF NAAFI shop *now*! It appears that your wife has caused some sort of an incident, and involved Cpl. Said. Bloodshed must be averted. GO NOW!"

So Warty at once went on his mission, having passed a hasty message to the Black Dwarf in case reinforcements were needed.

Arriving in the NAAFI, Warty found Dr. D. in a typical volatile Central European rage with intermittent tears, and being characteristically noisy, with Cpl Said, angry and proud, in the act of pinning the terrified manager to the wall by the muzzle of his rifle, clearly loaded, cocked, and ready to fire.

Warty calmed down all three and ascertained what had happened. Dr. D., quite properly entitled as the wife of a serving British Officer to use the shop facilities, had asked Cpl. Said to drive her there to purchase certain necessary feminine articles not available in the local market. At the checkout, the manager, not realising her status, and failing to check it, had briskly and unwisely told her that she could not use the shop and must leave. When she refused so to do, he compounded his error—and potential misfortune—by gently taking her arm to steer her to the exit. This elicited a violent reaction from the devout Muslim Cpl. Said. As he explained to Warty, "Sahib, this unclean dog of a Hindu grabbed our Memsahib and pushed her! So it was but my sworn duty to protect her and teach him manners and proper respect."

In the face of such traditional fierce loyalty, Warty was nonplussed. While reluctant to cause a fresh outburst of Central European volatility and histrionics, or to be seen as favouring Muslim over Hindu, he had to find some way to defuse the situation and ease himself off the horns of a particularly sharp dilemma.

Relief came in the form of the Black Dwarf (himself a Royal Military Police Officer), and two burly RAF Police Corporals. Under the Black Dwarf's direction, they arrested Cpl. Said on a charge of causing a disturbance, and the manager on a charge of minor assault. They left the fate of Dr. D. to Warty, who sought and took the advice of the Brigadier's wife, and put her, still protesting loudly, on the next available flight back to UK.

Honour having been satisfied all round, Warty and the Black Dwarf reported the conclusion to the Brigadier. The gallant Cpl. Said spent some four hours in custody, after which token punishment he was released by Warty to resume his driving duties.

11

Monkey's Missile

The Powers That Be, in their Infinite Wisdom, decreed that Warty's Battery should have a change of role. Although still to be based in the grim former Wehrmacht barracks in Sennelager, it had to hand in its beloved guns and revert to the anti-tank role which it last had in North Africa in 1942, when members of the current NATO Alliance were being somewhat less well inclined to each other than now. They therefore took over from the Cavalry (who showed a certain ill-grace, they felt) the magnificent, if somewhat erratic "Swingfire" Long range anti-tank missile system. Since each missile cost about the same as a top range civilian car, live firings were limited by an ever-parsimonious MoD, so to enable them to practise "hands-on", they were issued with two dummy training missiles. Naturally, custody of these important Stores items devolved upon Monkey, who duly took them on charge, and planned to keep them secure in his basement empire. He had, of course, not reckoned on the ingrained penchant of all true BSMs to paint, polish, and display, and very soon lost one of his missiles to the clutches of Battery Sergeant Major Charmes, who, having approved the burnishing of said missile, had it mounted proudly at the entrance of the Battery Block, pointing vaguely east, but more particularly aimed directly at the main entrance to the Cavalry Regiment's Officers' Mess.

It so happened that Warty's brother, an Officer in the Royal Navy, was at the time commanding one of Her Majesty's warships, moored in Bremerhaven, engaged on a liaison visit to the NATO Baltic Squadron. Since Bremerhaven was but a couple of hours drive up the Autobahn, what could be more natural than for a fraternal visit to be arranged for the two units to enjoy a weekend of sport, relaxation and jollity? The Battery braced itself. Thirty or so Jolly Tars duly arrived, were fed, watered and shown their bunks prior to changing dress for sporting contents.

The Battery history does not relate who won these, and also draws a kindly and discreet veil over the celebrations in the Battery Club later that evening. Suffice to say that the Battery Senior Ranks team, led by BSM Charms and our old friend Monkey, nobly and heroically engaged in such pursuits as "High Cockalorum", "Cardinal Puff", Mess Rugby, and similar.

Next morning, after the tardy and subdued departure of the Jack Tars to return to their "Tupperware" Minehunter, to Monkey's incoherent rage and impotent fury, the dummy training "Swingfire" on display at the entrance was found to be missing, presumed en route north to Bremerhaven.

Despite a flurry of "Immediate" signals, representations at the highest level, even an appeal to the First Sea Lord, the missile was never found and the culprits never admitted its removal.

However, some months later, MI6 started to get very strange reports that the Soviet Spy Agencies had tasked their agents in Eastern Europe to investigate and identify, as a matter of greatest urgency, the nature of a new British Royal Navy weapon, possibly a state-of-the-art Ship-to-Ship missile, photographed by their spy satellite mounted on the foredeck of a British Minehunter deployed in the Baltic.

When Warty told him of this, Monkey took a certain grim satisfaction in the confusion caused to Her Majesty's enemies. However, he continued to mourn the loss of Monkey's Missile, and never forgave the Royal Navy or Warty's brother.

12

Warty Dispenses Justice

After many years of service Warty had reached the exalted rank of Major and had been rewarded with command of his own Battery. His responsibilities included acting as a Magistrate, being charged with the "maintenance of Good Order and Military Discipline" as the Army Act 1955 described it. In the 1980s, one of the curses of military life in BAOR was absenteeism, soldiers going AWOL for periods, causing havoc to plans and routines, and placing an unfair extra workload on other members of the Battery. Warty was determined that his Battery would not suffer from the disruption that AWOL caused and carefully explained to the assembled all ranks that

a. This was an unacceptable offence, up with which he would not put.

b. Absence was unnecessary since Battery Sergeant Major "Bobo" Charmes would look with a kindly and sympathetic eye upon any genuine request for leave.

He resolved to deal as firmly as he was legally able with anyone found guilty, firmly supported by BSM Charmes.

One of the largest, blackest, and most popular NCOs in the Battery was Winston "Benny" Industrious, whose family, now in London, came originally from Grenada, in the West Indies. Some 18 stone of powerful and agile lean muscle and bone, he was the mainstay of the Battery's Rugby and Athletic teams, and the terror and despair of any other heavyweight boxer matched against him at Regimental, Brigade, or even BAOR level. Few challenged him, and fewer survived such a challenge. He was a potent force within the Battery, in barracks, or in the Field. Liked by most and respected by all.

Benny's troop commander was a languid and somewhat louche young Captain called Christopher-Robin Applebey, invariably addressed as CR. His main claim to fame was his attractive Belgian wife Annette, whose amazing bosom made her extremely popular with all the other officers, if not their wives, who openly and cattily speculated about silicone enhancement. The males just wished that they were in the position to make their own survey and judgement.

Putting these matters sternly to one side, it was with firm military resolve (although not a little trepidation), that Warty, having found Benny "guilty as charged" of one day's absence without leave (in order to visit his totally gorgeous brown-skinned girlfriend Monique, who was living "pro-tem" in Dortmund), fined the said Battery Hero the sum of £50, Benny having courteously but firmly rejected Warty's offer of trial by Higher Authority. Despite some minor muted mutterings, the Battery accepted the essential fairness of this treatment of its favourite son.

Warty's reputation of "firm but fair" was further enhanced the next day, when he conducted a lively and forthright interview with CR Appleby, who had tried to "test the system" (and Warty's patience) by taking an unauthorised day off to escort the pneumatic Annette on a shopping trip. Warty had no mercy, and indicated that he would fine CR £50 as well. CR then had the gall to tell Warty that a Major had no legal power to impose a fine on an Officer. "True" conceded Warty, "but unless I have your voluntary cheque in favour of the regimental Charity Fund on my desk within five minutes, you will be in front of a Court Martial before the month ends."

The Battery, discreetly briefed on this by BSM Bobo, who of course had been glued to the communication hatch between his office and Warty's, was delighted and much pleased. Justice had been done, and seen to be done.

There would be no further cases of AWOL during the remainder of the Battery's tour of duty in BAOR.

13

Warty the Cat Smuggler

After the adventures related in 'Warty all at Sea' and 'A Haunted Night', Warty had "bought out" Ron and the Black Dwarf and had brought *Sundance* safely back to UK waters, and arranged a berth for her in the new marina at Ramsgate, conveniently close to Folkstone, where he was now posted as a staff officer. Sharing his Army Married Quarter with him and his family were their two cats, 'Sanoor' and 'Thomas', both elegant longhaired Persians. Sanoor was already an experienced sea-cat, having spent several days and nights aboard *Sundance* in various marinas—once, while in Brighton Marina, causing great alarm to an elderly sleeping yachtsman by jumping through his open fore hatch, and landing on his chest. His cry of alarm as he awoke, startled, to the vision of yellow feline eyes, sat up and banged his head on the coach roof, was truly pitiful to hear. Warty, of course, snored on, blissfully unaware of Sanoor's nocturnal prowling. However, Fate paid him back.

One fine weekend he decided to take *Sundance* out for a day's mackerel fishing. The family car was loaded early, complete with Sanoor, securely locked in her travelling cat carrier. They had a very successful day, the fishing helped by an enthusiastic Sanoor. Arriving back late evening to Ramsgate marina, Warty and family decided to get a few hours sleep, returning to Folkestone in the early hours of the next morning, ready for Warty to change into uniform, in good time for First Parade in the barracks. So, as dawn was just breaking, Warty started to move the family bags (and bucket of mackerel) from *Sundance* to the car on the quayside, about 50 feet above the marina pontoon. He decided to start with Sanoor, in her cat-basket. Normally quite docile whilst travelling, she decided she didn't want to leave the boat and expressed her displeasure very vocally indeed. Warty, however, managed to disregard the howling and screeching and carried the cat box up the vertical ladder from the pontoon to the car park, and locked her securely in the car, still safe in her cat box, while he made three more trips for the rest of the luggage. This task finished, he thankfully secured *Sundance*, climbed the ladder for the final time and drove off towards Folkestone, still smelling faintly of mackerel.

About ten miles out of town blue flashing lights ahead and high visibility signs indicated a Police roadblock. Puzzled, Warty dutifully slowed to a halt, wound down his window and answered the questions from one of Kent's Finest. Where was he going? From where had he come? Did he realise the severe penalties for the illegal landing in the UK of animals from abroad in contravention of the "Prevention of Rabies" Legislation? With some difficulty, Warty persuaded Mr Plod that

a. he had not been outside the three-mile limit,

b. he needed to get to the Barracks in time for First Parade, and

c. he had merely taken his cat for a day's fishing.

Mr Plod, having licked the lead of his pencil a final time, and snapped his notebook closed, agreed that Warty was not, in fact, a cat smuggler (as suggested by a concerned and public-spirited yachtsman who had seen—and heard—them departing from the Marina, and had phoned HM Customs). Warty therefore started to continue his journey home. Sanoor, however, still vocal and unhappy, had managed to escape from her box into the car, and from there jumped out of the open window, evaded the startled Plod, and made good her escape into the nearby field. It took 3 hours, 10 policemen and about 20 motorists pressed into temporary service to catch her.

Warty was late for parade. The Brigadier was cross. The mackerel, however, cooked on Warty's barbecue later that evening were delicious. Sanoor even allowed Thomas a small share.

14

Warty and The Black Dwarf Sail Again

His day's fishing trip offshore had rekindled Warty's love of sailing. He therefore took advantage of the Black Dwarf's presence in the UK on a long course (and being at last comfortable in using his recently discovered first name, David) to invite him, as a trusted and tried shipmate, to come for a sail over a long weekend break to the Channel Islands and back. This was not without its hazards, the waters around the Channel Islands being begirt with jagged and vicious rocks, and the tidal streams fierce. However he was confident that the combination of his experience and offshore navigation skill, allied with Dave's superb inshore piloting, would cope. So, with favourable weather forecast, they set off from the Solent, to where they had repositioned *Sundance* from Ramsgate and out into the English Channel. Having crossed the Separation Lanes safely (as fast as possible and at right angles to the traffic flow, as decreed by HM Coastguard), they made a fast passage and a good landfall in Braye Harbour, Alderney. There they paused for rest and refreshment, going ashore in the dinghy to test the beer in the "Harbour Lights". It proved to be very acceptable and the two friends passed a peaceful night with comfortable sleep.

The next morning, after a hearty military breakfast, Warty consulted the Nautical Almanac, judged the tide times correctly, and they were soon underway for Guernsey. But, after about an hour, Warty began to get increasingly nervous. Not only was the weather getting worse, with thick clouds and regular heavy rain-showers reducing visability and making position fixing difficult, but he sensed that their speed seemed to be increasing. Warty asked Dave to come on deck and observe, which he did, reporting from the foredeck that "mini whirlpools" could be seen both to Port and Starboard. Disappearing below again, he then reappeared triumphant, reporting to Warty that the "whirls" were clearly marked on the chart and mentioned in the Pilot books. They were caught, luckily going in the right direction, in the infamous "Alderney Race", and approaching Guernsey at more than ten knots, even without the benefit of engine or sail power.

Luckily, the weather cleared, allowing both Warty and Dave to get a good position fix and identify the indistinct leading marks into Beaucette Marina.

Even so, the approach channel was narrow, with vicious rocks on both sides. Since dusk was now falling, once again the intrepid Dave had to go "forrard" with a powerful torch, to illuminate the rocks and shout course (and sometimes coarse!) corrections to Warty, who finally thankfully steered *Sundance* through the extremely narrow entrance to the Marina (at one time a stone quarry, with an entrance to the sea created by blasting through the cliff), and to a calm and comfortable pontoon berth. And oh! What joy! A decent-looking restaurant and bar within staggering distance! It was thoroughly tested that evening. Both Warty and the Black Dwarf felt they deserved it, so they scoffed Guernsey lobster, and toasted "Absent Friends" in cold French Sauvignon blanc.

15

Many A Good Tune (Warty Remembers)

Although still pretty active, Warty was getting older, greyer, and, like a good wine, more mature, and, like many similar old gents, liked to remember the exploits of his youth. One of his favourite memories included his old chum "Bullet" (the nickname given for his lethal speed on the Rugby pitch), Jannie Rhodie-Stansberg, a member of the African White Tribe, who had been sent by his Government for Officer training at the RMA Sandhurst.

The University of Reading enjoys a justifiable very fine academic reputation. In the early sixties, however, this was not its principal attraction for Warty, and Bullet, then serving together as Officer Cadets at the reasonably nearby Royal Military Academy, Sandhurst. To them, the main object of interest was the large resident student population, half of which were those magical creatures with bumpy sweaters—Girls! To fit and healthy young men immured for long periods in the austere and monastic surroundings of the Academy, the University held a promise of clearly defined, much desired, and just achievable untold pleasure.

Mrs Beldon, the resident Warden of the Women's Hall of Residence, was an outwardly stern and sturdily-built lady, whose bulldog-like countenance and grimly permed hair struck fear into any of the young women—or their erstwhile boyfriends—who transgressed against her appointed role as moral guardian. She was also, somewhat surprisingly, an accomplished pianist, whose pride and joy, an ancient but much cherished and well-tuned upright piano, stood in the Hall Common room under the window where the light was best.

Warty and "Bullet" had been invited to the University Summer Ball as guests of two young lady students of Warty's acquaintance. Somewhat over refreshed, the girls had decided that the merrymaking should continue in the more private and congenial venues of their rooms in the Hall of Residence. Thus it was that Warty awoke with a start very late in the evening to realise that there was grave danger of missing the last train back to Sandhurst. Accordingly, he dressed, stumbled down a dark and unfamiliar corridor and by great good fortune found the room where Bullet and his partner for the evening were ensconced in mutual admiration. "Quick, Bullet," he hissed, "we've really got to get a move on! The last train goes in twenty minutes and if we miss it we are deep in the mire with the Sergeant-Major!" Followed by a sleepy Bullet, hopping on one leg as he pulled on his trousers, he fled down the stairs to the main door. Horror! It had been locked and barred by the ever-vigilant Mrs Beldon. Back up the stairs they tore to the Common Room, where, to their relief, they found they could open the window over the piano from where it was but a short drop to the lawn below.

So they climbed onto the piano and leaped into the dark, both landing safely, but to a resounding crashing noise from within the Hall. The noise brought most of the lights on, and Mrs Beldon's enraged features leaning out of her window, shaking her muscular fist at our Heroes as they legged it down the road towards the station. Bullet, in his leap, had pushed over the piano! Mrs Beldon's pride and joy was never again to sound forth.

Warty and Bullet, however, caught the train in time, and courtesy of a comradely Guard Commander, managed to sneak into the Academy just before the appointed Witching Hour.

They, and the delicious and enterprising young ladies, reckoned that the demise of Mrs Beldon's piano was well worth such a pleasant evening, especially since the foursome had greatly enjoyed sweet music of a quite different and more exquisite nature altogether.

16

Castles In Spain

Major (Retd.) "Warty" Nasty-Farting, VD and Scar, an ancient British Gunner, very much liked to drink beer, as his shape attested. He had sampled most brands during his many years of "long service in hot climates". He and his companion, Brigadier (Retd.) Jannie "Bullet" Rhodie-Stansberg, an equally Ancient Warrior of the African White Tribe, were particularly fond of "Castle" Lager, a brew familiar to all those who have served in Central and Southern Africa.

However, none was currently available, so they were consoling themselves with draught "San Miguel", the local brew in the high class resort where the battle-weary, scarred, and hardened Ancient Heroes, clearly long-time friends and military colleagues now retired from Active Service, were enjoying a well deserved holiday in the sun in the company of Trish and Hazel, their toothsome (and younger) wives.

Once long ago both blond-eyed, blue-haired Nordic Gods, they were semi-submerged in the Jacuzzi on the patio of the self-catering apartment, and rapidly turning "Rooinek" red in the Spanish sun, even Bullet.

"I say, Old Bullet," said Warty, "just look at the state of that" (eyeing some delicious bikini-clad young stuff joggling past. "Not many of those to the pound, eh?"

"Certainly at least two standard British handfuls!"

"Aagh, man," came the jaded response. "Calm down, you're making the water spill over. Besides, the wives will soon be back from their shopping trip to Marbella, and they'll take a sjambok to us both!"

"Okay, ou maat," said Warty cheerfully. "Then let's have a beer to cool us down and get the body fluid up to the correct level." Spotting Diego Garcia, the distinctly limp-wristed Spanish duty waiter hovering nearby, Warty's stentorian military voice summoned him: "Diego" (pronounced "Dago") "you wretch! *Dos cervezas por favor!* Two beers please!"

The response *"Si Senor, pronto!"* was immediate. Two small beers, very cold, arrived with but a short delay.

Warty was almost beside himself and incoherent with rage. "Dago! You, you, limp-wristed, panty-waisted excuse for a Spic! These are small beer—pequeno cervezas! Do you think that El Generale Bullet here is *uno marisco* like you? He drinks only big beers—*grande cevezas!* Get two big beers now—now, or I'll fry your cojones on the barbecue!"

Diego, much concerned, retreated at speed, mindful of the occasion when one of his colleagues who had previously displeased our heroes had been hurled bodily across the patio and lawn into the swimming pool. He soon returned, bearing very large beers to placate the comrades. Warty drank deeply. "Aah, that's better." He farted joyfully, unnoticed in the Jacuzzi bubbles.

"Chraast, Warty," said Bullet, "Heads down, here come the girlies. Looks like they had a good raid on the shops."

Trish and Hazel entered daintily, heavy laden with smart carrier bags. "Hi boys! Look what we've bought! New FMPs, pretty lacy things and smashin' handbags. Terrible thirsty work, though!"

"Humph!" Jointly and grumpily said Warty and Bullet. "Hope we can still afford to buy you a drink!" Then they relented, and together yelled: "Dago!"

Peace reigned throughout the subsequent impromptu Fashion Show. Dinner, however, much later, was an altogether much more lively affair.

17

Warty Saves the Day in Africa

Warty had gone to Zimbabwe to spend some time with his old friends Jannie and Hazel Rhodie-Stansberg. Jannie and the fragrant Hazel lived in Bulawayo, about five miles from the Government State House, built on the site of the Kraal where Lobengula, the last Matabele King, had held court.

Despite the deepening political and economic crisis gripping that unhappy land, Warty and Jannie had even more serious concerns. Their home stock of "Castle" Lager was fast dwindling and the problem of resupply in a thirsty land rapidly becoming acute, so, over dinner, a plan was hatched, and, next day put into effect. Warty, at the head of a "mini-impi" of ten stalwart Matabeles, led by the grizzled Sevico, now Hazel's head gardener, but still a scion of his warrior tribe, steeped in the history and legends of his people and their victories in battle, set off in Jannie's pick-up truck for the nearest bottle store in downtown Bulawayo. The impi, grinning broadly, squatted in the back and made loud and cheerful noises, especially when passing full-bosomed and wide-beamed Matabele maidens, who were subjected to broad-humoured although good-natured comments and invitations.

The bottle store reached, Warty, Sevico and two warriors alighted, leaving the remainder to guard the pickup. Into the store they went, to be greeted by a woeful-looking owner, Mr Patel. Horrors! No beer was to be had, he claimed, dejectedly, gesturing to the empty shelves. Warty, however, was not an old soldier for nothing. A certain handshake was gripped, quiet words were cautiously spoken, and foreign currency notes discreetly pressed into the Indian palm.

A cunningly disguised door to a rear storeroom swung open, and crates of Castle Lager carried out to the waiting pickup, where a jubilant mini-impi chanted victory songs and praises to Warty, clearly a mighty warrior and Induna of the Great White Queen over the water. This went on until home was reached.

Thirst, like Mafeking and Ladysmith, had been relieved, and all that night "joy was unconfined and celebration thrived!"

18

Warty Returns to Spain

Warty was fed-up. Not deeply unhappy, but miserable enough to upset his normal bluff, hearty and cheerful equilibrium for which he was well known.

He was sitting at a table near the bar beside the pool, where Bullet and he had sat before. This year, however, he was alone. Bereft of his toothsome and beloved Trish, and with Bullet and Hazel effectively trapped in Africa, Warty had decided to test the system, and in so doing, sample some Spanish sunshine away from Blighty's rain.

Two glasses of the local red wine had blunted the edge of his emotional pain. His physical discomfort, however, persisted. The first major challenge, the flight and journey from the UK, had gone well, thanks to 30 years of military experience. Likewise, challenge 2—an electrical power failure throughout all southern Spain—had been overcome, with the aid of his ever trusty military torch and three candles supplied by the resort.

Even when he misplaced his spectacles, Warty didn't panic. Without a female to assist in the search, like most males, Warty, of course, "couldn't see for looking". However, the ever-helpful girls at Reception swiftly despatched a female cleaner who found them in about 30 seconds (in the bathroom, carefully and safely placed where clumsy Warty was less likely to smash them).

The next challenge was, however, rather more serious. Increasing discomfort developed into a distinct and painful boil between Warty's buttocks! Such things, although by no means medical emergencies, can be uncomfortable enough to need urgent medical advice, if not treatment. Having taken all sensible practical measures, again learned during many years of long service in hot climates, Warty decided to summon the local medico who duly arranged an appointment for the next morning.

Although Warty's crude but effective self-treatment worked, and the situation resolved itself, somewhat messily, overnight, Warty decided not to cancel the medical visit. Order and counter order led to disorder, he recalled.

But Horror! Not only was the doctor a young and pretty female—not the sort of person Warty relished peering between his leathery military buttocks, but she was accompanied by an even younger doe-eyed and distinctly limp-wristed Spanish male assistant to carry her bag.

Mildly apprehensive when the doctor snapped on long rubber gloves prior to her examination, Warty became decidedly alarmed when the assistant also snapped on gloves and indicated that Warty should "assume the position" on the bed.

Of course, matters proceeded perfectly professionally. The assistant remained outside while the doctor examined, confirmed Warty's diagnosis and successful self-treatment, applied ointment, and departed rejoicing, 50 Euros richer, courtesy of the Health Insurance Company.

Warty's somewhat laboured attempt at humour in suggesting that having been so intimate, she would now have to marry him, was firmly rejected. He was, she told him somewhat crisply, too late. She was already married to an eminent local surgeon who, in his youth, had been the light heavyweight boxing champion for Andalucia Province.

POSTSCRIPT: 'Old Comrades'—A poem for Warty and Bullet

A long time ago in the Eifel,[1] both Warty and Bullet were there.
Slimmer, perhaps, and more agile
With definitely more golden hair.

The final great Summer Manoeuvre
Their RMA course at an end
Just Sovereign's Parade lay before them,
Before different ways they must wend.
The hot summer sunshine had bronzed them,
Their Mess Dress was fitted and pressed,
For the Commissioning Ball up in London,
The Dorchester looked at its best.
Their Regiments welcomed the Heroes,
To Germany Warty was sent.
While Bullet returned to Rhodesia,
To live in the veldt in a tent.
Now forty years later, the comrades,
Bemedalled and scarred and quite grey,
Are sitting in Spain, sipping lager, and yarning of old yesterday
When things seemed much simpler and clearer,
And soldering really great fun,

1. The Eifel Mountains in Germany were the location of the final exercise for Warty and Bullet's intake of Officer Cadets at RMA Sandhurst, prior to the final formal parade ("Sovereign's Parade), which was followed by a ball at the Dorchester Hotel, and then, as young Officers, dispersal to their Regiments.

A worthwhile career in the Service.
Of getting the "terrs" on the run.
For many years both served their Countries
And kept in close touch with their friend,
In good times and bad times together,
Staunch, loyal, and true to the end.
Now Warty and Bullet are hoping,
Ere joining the Great Mess Above,
To drink many Castles[2] together,
Till the trumpet call sounds "It's enough!"

THE END

2. References to "sipping lager together 40 years later", and "Castles", are explained in various chapters.

About the Author

After attending and graduating from the Royal Military Academy, Sandhurst, the author was Commissioned into the Royal Regiment of Artillery in 1963, and completed a full career as a Regular Army Officer until1989, serving in the British Army of the Rhine, Oman, where he saw active service against the Communist insurgents, and Rhodesia/Zimbabwe. During these years he held a wide variety of posts, both at Regimental duty and on the Staff, including Command of "J" (Sidi Rezegh) Battery, Royal Horse Artillery, an Independent battery armed with "Swingfire" long-range antitank missiles, launched from tracked armoured vehicles. He was a keen offshore yachtsman, and a highly experienced and qualified underwater diver, being appointed a Joint Service Subaqua Diving Supervisor. In 1974, he was awarded HM the Sultan of Oman's Commendation for the action described in "Warty's oilrig". In 1991, he was recruited by the Commanding Officer of the 4th (TA) Battalion of the Devon and Dorset Regiment (his grandfather's Regiment), to command Headquarter Company, based in Exeter, Devon, a post that he held until 1993, when a stroke suffered while on duty overseas led to his retirement on disability grounds. He is divorced, and still lives in Exeter, working as a voluntary welfare caseworker for the Royal British Legion and a fundraiser for the Army Benevolent Fund. Other interests include teaching the German language, in which he is almost bilingual, and writing.

978-0-595-48300-6
0-595-48300-3

Printed in the United Kingdom
by Lightning Source UK Ltd.
126741UK00001B/415-462/A

9 780595 483006